The Year There Were
No Apples

The Year There Were No Apples

Poems by James A. LaFond-Lewis

CW Books

Published by CW Books
P.O. Box 541106
Cincinnati, OH 45254-1106

ISBN: 9781625491978

Poetry Editor: Kevin Walzer
Business Editor: Lori Jareo

Visit us on the web at www.readcwbooks.com
Author's website: jimlewis.net

Cover Photo by the author.
Author photo: self portrait.

Thank You

To the Jamaica Pond Poets,
Dorothy Derifield, Carolyn Gregory,
Holly Guran, Audrey Henderson, Susanna Kittredge,
Alice Kociemba, Dorian Kotsiopoulos,
Jennifer Markell, Sybille Rex,
Alan Smith Soto, Sandra Storey and Gary Whited.
They each have given me the benefit of their
experience and sensibilities, their talent, their sharp
eyes and ears and best of all,
their boundless good will, a man's only real treasure.

To my family, friends and coworkers who encourage
me to explore the unique inner workings of my
individual mind and heart while simultaneously
deepening the connections between and among us.
My audience, the wide sea of poets,
sitting in rows on hard backed benches and folding
chairs.
Everyone a harbor.
We are nothing without each other.

To Cheryl

Table of Contents

Fallow

I've been wandering
in the bare orchard,
trees like twisted wire,
knuckle grafts exposed,
apples merely memories,
promises from past seasons,
stones sucking cold from air,
matted grass laying for snow,
prints from house to barn
bald as sunset.

When the Crows Came

I fell in love with their
shiny blue black
their bouncing haunches
and their wisecracks.

I grew impatient with their distrust
and their off-the-cuff remarks.

I thought I might learn
to tell them apart
but I only succeeded
in making myself
an odd sort of human.

Growl

We were out walking our gods
when, no surprise,
they growled at each other.

I held mine
and you yours
but not before mine
circled wide around
and yours snapped
and snarled at me
and mine.

Whispers

Let's get this straight, I am
not much but I am
God's neighbor
and there's a skunk
that lives between us
who wanders around my garage
and has sprayed my dog.

Today I heard whispers
from under the car
telling me to write
and now I'm afraid to leave the house.

Signature

She went around the world backwards,
"So that's where I was."
she said as the wind whipped 'round her hair,
carrying the future rearward,
the afterwards were sucked out like credits,
like dusk,
like the signature on the painting,
nothing like the painting.
"Did you see that day? I was in that sunset."

Beekeeper

Because you are a warrior woman,
kin of the African queen,
I want to gentle you,
all that honey,
perfect combs.

I'm on your landing board
your narrow entrance
turned toward the sun,
our secret flowers
and the buzz
that follows you,
all those useless drones.

I Went Looking for the Muse

I don't know why.
When she's ready
she pounds on my door.
I'm rolled out of bed at odd hours,
stray thoughts in the street
commanded at pen-point
worry about keeping my head, never mind my clothes
which might easily be kicked under the bed,
thrown in the tub, abandoned in the cellarway
near the potatoes and onions,
might not feel like a head at all,
but more like a cabbage or a Brussels sprout
and even peeled, skinned,
I love when she rolls me.

She'll find me in the face of a woman not my wife
or in a dream not my own
and she'll rattle me, throttle me until I spill
drooling like an old fool
and no one there to wipe my face
sometimes a bad smell
and though I might repel myself
I don't regret her
until she leaves,
she always leaves,
the rich lady with the long legs.

True Romance

English is a fair, generous woman
who can't confine herself
to one steadfast man.
She craves every raven haired
romance with any land
foreign or far
filled with struggle
and strange rooms,
cryptic, incomprehensible
except by sounds and gestures
that linger in her dreams
teeth and tongue cleaved
white and red
any bastard word
her legitimate dark eyed child.

Biography

When you write your life story
make your villain look like me.
Make his eyes compel you
and his hands
the hands you fear
will not touch you.

When you get to the foolishness
that defies convention
bring me to life
in the man you're afraid not to love.

When you throw it all away
hold me like your last coin
and squeeze me
until I stick
to the sweat in your palm.

And when it's time to kiss goodbye,
kiss me as if goodbye is all you have
to say how much you've lost.

A Woman in Love

is a hand unclenched
fingers spread, palm flung open
from the wrist.

Out of love
a fist clenched
down to the toes.

The Reading

In the second row on the aisle
a woman I had never seen

looked across the ocean
between us

Her eyes were a long voyage
returned from a storm

I red for her
I right for her

a deep harbor she sailed into
through the reading

Inarticulate Boy

There was a time,
most of my life,
when I fell in love easily,
when a zephyr blew
or a tidal pool warmed itself in the sun
beside a cold ocean
when a girl looked into me and held my gaze
until she was inside and I was inside out
on the verge of understanding...
what?

I live in this world where weather is made
and waves crash and sometimes
I am a reluctant sailor.
Some women, deep in the eyes,
look like harbors.

On the Rocks

I held my breath
dove into her deep eyes
and swam to the shallow end,
out through the cracked red
of her enameled toes.

Dear Poet

I want the air between us
to come unkempt and disorderly
so you'll sing your songs for me.

I want you
to feel yourself stroked
by the backs of my fingers
as if by horsehair strung
on Pernambuco wood

frets raised to my fingertips.
I want to leave you
and get surreptitious notice
that a love lyric
has jumped up on the web,

Signed.

I want to see red
and be soothed.

I want you to love me secretly, in public,
the sounds drifting across campus
and up the highway.

I want to be the pond
where your hymns go naked to swim.

Controlled Substance

I want to be under the influence
of a sunset
that cuts through dark November
as if it was August

like a blind dog on a mission from here to there,
compelled by scent.

I want to be under the influence of billions of stars,
on a narrow path littered with light,
no moon, no dog baying.

I want to be under the influence of
drink so stiff that my tongue hangs
and drips words.

I want to be under the influence of
mysteries that feel like wads of cash
and bars of silver in someone else's possession.

I want to be under the influence of a woman
who is under my influence,
her skin a controlled substance,
her desire a stimulant not yet banned,
her sweat a reward,
her legs.

Earth

When we have shucked our clothing
onto cool wood floors,
a slight draft raising our skin,
and you stand unabashed in warm sunlight,
ripe, like crimson grapes,
with my fingers like vines rising up from the sand,
I will reach into the air that surrounds you.

And I will give
a gentle tug to hanging fruit,
until it presses wet into my hands,
and the lush earth fills my nose,
I can no longer stand,
but kneel before this crop
and with my thumb inside the earth herself,
taste what only she provides.

She Flew the Atlantic

There was her husband
who'd conceded, me,
and a man from elsewhere, U.S.A.
whose mention alone raised my hackles.

I wrote the words,
on which she flew the Atlantic,
no more.

For a moment,
my head
that I'd been spinning out for heart
easily given, was easily won.

She came,
parlayed,
but would not keep it.

Making Soup

With knife in hand,
stems and roots and leaves
pulled from the ground and peeled,
remembering a woman I followed
when she smiled at me over her shoulder,
to the bare wood behind her house
stood beside her and surveyed
the scrub lot and leafless brush,
an old bicycle on weeds that couldn't pass for lawn,
broken clay pot, black bucket tired with mud,
newspapers and magazines rotted together,
once soft, now hard and aslant,
a page of blue bled into the ground,
paper flaked and glued all around her paradise,
she pointed to a tomato plant and sequestered herbs
and touched my face which reminds me now, I want
her in my soup, wildflowers gone to thorns,
sauntering into the house, me trailing
through a door that yaws open, slams shut
she suggested tea, black and sweet
all the chairs covered with junk, the counter littered,
a sweep of her arm sending plates to the floor,
startling me to wonder about clothing,
where to stand, though now I'm standing
at my own sink, orderly and clean,
with celery, carrots and onions, diced to tears.
We leaned into the corner, our arms
wrapped, her pelvis pressed against my leg,
her warmth seeping into my groin,
and now the soup beginning to steam.

Black Widow

I met a woman who has been married twice,
now she has lost patience with her second husband
and the next one hasn't yet been chosen.

Thankfully,
I failed the audition:
not enough money,
too much wife,
no ambition.

Wrinkled Man

He leaks tears on pristine linens
stamped with "property of" and woven with
blue and pink stripes,
a basin at his bedside,
finite breaths, unsudden gaps,
torn saliva strings,
dying long ahead,
while a woman kneels beside
counting all ten fingers and toes,
to the rhythm of the oxygen
tsss... tsss... tsss...
wondering when they will go home.

On Horse Mountain

My girl and I went past infrequent houses
to the Maine woods, long gashes of lumbered land,
dense forest cleanly sliced by hard dirt roads,

the only ones climbing up or down
Horse Mountain until joined at the top
by a man who'd run up after us
breathing hard, hollow and dry,
cigarette wrapper skin, white eyes sped black
with ash that wouldn't settle.

We stood in the fire tower
while he dug into the wood,
jagged epithets, a name, a date,
deep cutting that hardened the cords of his arms,
fresh scars that threatened everything.
We dared not look closely.

My girl and I clambered
down to an outcrop of stone,
forcing our backs to him
while we shared a picnic lunch.
He followed and demanded a sandwich.
We gave him half.
He took a bite, hacked it in two,
whipped the rest over the hill
where it fell apart against the rocks
and stuck,
as if ours was the insult.

Shotgun

When we were passengers
in a car driven by a freaking ghost
we stared at him, and then each other.
His skin drained white,
his mouth gone wide,
he burst into a sound I'd heard once,
the shrieking wail
my father blamed on a rabbit
about to become prey,
silence overwhelmed by terror.

Each of us begged him to brake,
but he accelerated.
If not for the narrow road
and descending evening
I might have convinced myself
we'd survive,
but in the fading light
his knuckles shone on the wheel,
the gray sky blurred,
rushed our heads,
the stone wall sudden and explosive.
Now we fear each other's eyes.

House of Worship

Now we fear the story
in each other's eyes
the jagged white,
the murky brown,
the frozen blue,
the tiny black,
dots
that drain
the basin empty
out the mouth, out the eyes,
out the massive brain case
where terrors are stored.

When

I'm seized by the pain of reading literature
with its careful eye toward heartbreak and truth
so many beginnings,
leading to so many middles
and so few endings,
as if there is a mountain in the distance
approached by myriad trails
climbing to the one peak
sad, and tall.

I can barely begin again
sometimes halting after a chapter
sometimes a page
lately even a line
like "the summer I turned ten"
or "in 1963"
and today it was just a word
"when."

"When" and I was done
the book in a heap of great ones
the word itself promising
lessons, sharp and dull,
sadness, keen and long,
death, sudden and eternal.

Aunt Mary

Uncle Larry went to opera
on long journeys and short afternoons
to the city or the local house
where the voices rang the iron in his blood
and the costumes lit the cones in his eyes.
Aunt Mary stayed home.

Aunt Mary .02

she was
a normal woman

who forgot
normally

who remembered forgetting so much
she frightened

until she forgot she forgot

and still normal
forgot what forgot meant

what a look was
what was is

who who is
what is a he

when who said
when was was.

woman doesn't know is is.

Mum

she saw
a boy
wasn't me
with a man
wasn't me
and fed herself ice
with the same bony hand
that she used to point
out where they stood
over my left shoulder

She was so lovely
when she smiled
at the sight
through my head
that I hoped she might really mean me.

Wrong Line

Ma died, slow quick,
friends murmur murmur
so sad to lose your mama
you must be off kilter.

It's true, but not like
after riding a merry-go-round
or wailing, no,
not like unmoored
or the ugly when Dad died
or when the driving man was crushed by a drunk,
not like when Gramma went
with memory crashed
to when cars were new inventions
the ice came daily
and a man shouted
from a pile of rags on a wagon,
no, not like untethered
or when the pretty dog laid down under the porch,
or the flowers wilted, faded, and dried.
Not like they think.

She diverted me,
like a train down the wrong line to the tracks' end,
pushed me, an overmatched ram, off high ground,
caught me against the windshield,
like a leaf in free fall and left me
somewhere I've never been.

Lady Slipper

There is no mistaking her footsteps
in hard high heeled shoes,
steady from a long way off,

but sometimes with mussed hair
in a silk robe she creeps up like sleep departing
on Sunday morning wearing pink slippers
she shuffles into my dream like a season
a little soft scraping that I mistake
for my father sucking on his unlit pipe
or my mother sliding pots across the stove
and then, even though my eyes are closed
and my breath is like a quiet engine
I see her smile as she approaches,
humming softly, dancing alone,
intent to take me with her,
I'm gripped by a fear I cannot name,
I'm naked, she's dressed,
I'm about to meet everyone I ever knew
and she has taken me to an empty room.

Since You Asked

Lately I've been coming apart,
hung on a string,
torn up the middle,
gunpowder green
bubbling out of a herniated bag
athwart compressed disk
leaking at the lining of my nerves
punctured on a sharp-boned foot.

I'd always thought
dying would be slow
like a teabag draining,
and so it was for my mother,
all water steeped.

But my father's
was a sudden squeeze,
two weeks of misery,
short. tight. neck.

Starting Point

After my father died
he took me up
like a banjo.
I've been singing all his songs.
Listening, too.
Everything front and back,
his and mine,
seeing the man,
and being,
his love of salt on sliced apple,
his absolute obeisance
and fear of love's power,
his discomfort with wealth,
his intellect as undertone
of joy, a weapon only in defense,
his easing terror of death,
his overwhelming inability to let go of self,
the warmth he couldn't speak,
the way that he worshiped
no god but my mother

all hollowed out
and strung
on me.

Bowed

I saw the trajectory of my life
in a stem bent by the weight of its flower
the flower dropping petals.

It Just Does

stars explode
liquids gas
dirts harden
sands melt
concretes crumble
knives dull
petals wilt
trees fall
voices fade
eyes blind
skins crack
bones break
brains forget
my heart
leaks

Every organization or loose association of
people ought to have its poet laureate

I would like to be poet laureate
of the Pervious Concrete Association.
I will meet regularly
with the members and the witch doctor.
We will all feel safe and uplifted
or grounded together.
We will mingle in the lobby before meetings.
I will dream enough for all of us,
especially during discussions
of the Maine Department of Transportation's RFPs.
I will draw attention to the sight and sound of
ME DOT RFP
and the doctor will conjure the rumble
a small airplane will make
as it rolls across a pervious runway in the rain.

Where once it would have been grounded,
bogged down in mud,
my poetry will rise off the concrete
and fly across Penobscot Bay!

Here's the Deal

You don't want to know me,
you want your driveway paved.

You don't want to tell stories
to your grandchildren
about the exploits of the
concrete salesman.

You don't want but seventy five per cent of my
material,
the other twenty five being hot air.

You don't want my friendship,
You want my pervious concrete.

alert

When the witch doctor stares at me
I pretend to be immune
but I'm cowed
by the intensity of his gaze;
I feel damp.
I smell myself
and sit rabbit still.

Devil's Door

I'm almost ashamed
of my dependence on the witch doctor,
the wild hair that halos his head
the dead white bone
the eloquent dance that means nothing
until he explains.

I realized today
the post nasal drip
that haunted me for years
has vanished and my favorite aunt
no longer seduces me in dreams.
I am not superstitious

nor is the doctor
so that when he told me to knock
on the devil's door every day at dusk,
I asked "What's the joke?"
He said that no devil needs a door
and he did a dance to demonstrate

how honeybees find nectar,
shaking his abdomen
in an ever widening circle
until my time was up.
I paid and left,
flying straight to the florist.

With Us in the Back, he Drives Away

the devil drives around ignorant
everywhere in a windowless van
and throws us in the back.

he smokes a stogie, binds us to him in filth
but even the white of extreme kindness
and the gray of love slightly askew
serve as his clouds.

he steals our bodies, snorts and shoots
but in the offing he sucks too hard
on his own cigar

shouts when we grab his neck
loses the wheel, but only shrugs and taunts
with what hoarse breath he has
no hands

in our impending death
we let go his immortal cancered throat
see clearly despite his face
only perfect compassion will save us.

Quabbin: Public Works

For decades, old clubs and congregations settled
into a native earthen vessel that would be dammed
at both its drains and flooded by the Swift.

Ancient hills became islands and pipers piped along
the Boston road. Uprooted souls, gnarled and knotty,
were pried away from their already dead,
dried old seeds numbered and re-interred
beyond water's reach, they continue not to grow.

Centuries of natives, deemed innumerable,
were left in muck below the concrete altars
that took their once sky.

After generations and a year of drought
rumors of an impossible church rising
out of the reservoir sent me to the water's edge
to survey the transubstantiated towns.

Below a clean horizon, they had from sticks
and bricks become elixir, a potable sea
of corners and centers and ends
submerged like toys by politicians.

Goodnough and Winsor, men and their dams,
left us the encircling Administration Road,
cellar holes, and a web of high asphalt streets
that square and crack across the watershed,
slope down empty, turn empty across the bottom
and rise on the opposite shore, empty.

A Vast White Sky

At sunrise,
a thin fog hangs
on Truman Highway.

The Neponset River lies
in a thigh-deep basin of chemical filth,
shoulders hunched under bridges,
an old osmotic sewer
left to its dark leeching
into weeds and trees.

But its vapor
haunts the hillside
caressing a flattened doe
whose timid eyes are gone to mud.

It lays up in doorways,
stickying porch lamps, veiling windows.

Everywhere sunlight weeps.

Gutter Repair

When you google the words "gutter repair"
and fill out the form, we are alerted.
An estimator is sent to your home,
who will make veiled references to the operation
as he makes a drawing of your house and takes
photographs.

He will then artfully defer
the genuine estimate to a third party.
We'll call him "the expert,"
who will climb a ladder
to tell you how much it will cost
to actually have your unique gutters repaired.

If you contract for gutter repair,
and perhaps downspout installation,
one third deposit is exacted,
scrutiny intensifies.

In any event,
your home's particulars
will be stored in the Langley cloud,
wires tapped,
satellite surveillance regularized
and your profile routinely updated.

The fact is, gutter repair is engaged
by a statistically-impossible percentage
of suspected terrorists
who own their own homes.

Once Upon a Time, a History

After the google wars,
when all perspective was once again bent,
and possession of people's online lives
overwhelmed the internet,
the spoils were taken
by those who would compel others,
who would plunder the treasury,
know everything about you,
exact your vote
make you pay.

After the google wars
privacy was outlawed,
only secrecy remained.

Child's Play

God is subject to His own commandments
and is ashamed of His own imperfections
which cascade down generations
like gangliosides of Tay-Sachs
hidden in the love of unsuspecting parents.
He makes infants and rattles them insensible until
dead.

Today

Today I might be a god
and nap
while they kill each other.
Lie in the sun
with my eyes closed
the warm rays on my back
or perhaps watch one
flay another
until his skin is gone
and feel the gentle breeze
ruffle the hair on the backs of my arms.
I might cry
or I might laugh at children
running into the ocean
or I might doze
while they do all of the things they do,
everywhere, always.

Across the Lot

I saw you from my back door across the vacant lot
pulling God up and over fences, heavy sucker
got stuck on barbed wire and toppled to the ground
you hanging on to his ears going down with him
left a bigger impression in the mud than I imagined.

Then I must have looked away, he was on your
shoulders, I could hear the sound of your shoes
as you pulled them up, suction cups like anchors,
me thinking, "Put him down, he wants to stay."

but you staggered up, God like a sack of potatoes, on
bent back, got to the road, so I stopped
talking to you and went straight for God,
"Leave him alone. Can't you see?"

He couldn't, his head down around your ass.
Your grip beginning to slip, God turned,
trained on me like there was something I could do,
then you were at the road, your legs straight,
you took three crooked steps, I recounted
when the police came asking.
I told them the truth through my tears
the driver was innocent, you staggered into the road,
with your heavy load, all God's fault.

Trespass Against Us

I was out fighting god one day, had him
in a head hold, smashing his skull against
a cement wall, and the blood,
(I never thought god would bleed so much)
was running down when I asked him to wait
and laid him down on the asphalt in the shade
then ran to get my camera, the blood so lovely
on the sun washed cement.

He smiled weakly when I got back because he knew
that I was worried he'd be gone. I was afraid
I'd have to wait until another day to finish him off,
but there he was smiling and I
got some very beautiful photographs
that reminded me of an old rusty building,
private property, keep out.

I was happy he was still there, wrapped my arms
around his neck again and got back to business
but his head felt warm against my chest, my heart
wasn't in the fight so I let him go.

He said that we'd see each other again,
I could kill him then, but I haven't seen him since.
I wonder if he died from his wounds.
Have any of you seen him?
Did I knock some sense into him?
Maybe you don't know him,
the arrogant one who ignores everyone
and does whatever he pleases.

Eye of a Needle

Beware my love,
it is not free.
It is wealth
in a sea of poverty,
health
on a planet of disease,
lettered
among profound illiteracy.
It requires you
to share
to heal
and to teach.

Ramshackle

When my devout Christian brother visits
my ramshackle soul
I wonder if he only sees the fallen down boards
and the tarpaper roof, the eaten bits littering the floor,
the stained mattress and its torn out ticking.

I wonder if he notices the chair,
its polished seat
sunlit in the early afternoon,
angled toward a crack in the wall,
a hobo's blackened hearth in the middle of the room
from where I can see the past, the old apple orchard,
lush fields where life began,
beyond the vats of rust and rainwater
to the frog ponds that made perfect skating,
connected as they were
by reedy trails through ice,
the lace curtain on the doorway
leading in and out,
and the ghost of me
seeing it again for the first time.

I wonder if he sees how found I am
and how much of me is love.

Old New England

You scoffed, the crackled teacup maiden
with her mother's antiques, her
financiers, archaeologists and engineers,
men in suspenders and straw hats
who dissected things with pens and brushes,
blew off the dust of centuries
only to watch it settle again
on the antimacassars she kept
on the chairs in the parlor.

I walked you along a stone wall,
strung like black pearls around an emerald field,
with stacks of whipped autumn hay
waiting to be eaten, turned
to anything but dust, and laid out in spring
on rows and mounds where slowly
in the month of July green gems grow
and suddenly in August
tomatoes, eggplants, peppers
and tall ears of corn pop
with filigreed threads.

You scoffed at brick hearths where pioneers
burned iron pots and arms and hands
and at wide cracked boards
where Shakers trimmed virtue into tables and desks
and dwindled and my grandfather hung on, just,
like the dry old clock in the corner,
telling broken time.

I showed you a boy
with a dog and a field and a forest
his head cocked to a hawk's screech,

his eye on life around the stream
that runs wet and high all year,
who struts, not for being seen,
but simply for being,
whose sense of humor is lit by the sky
with its different tricks of color
and the knowledge that no boy
has ever been right there right then
and who knows the crackle on the teacup house
is just the trail that time has taken.

American Slaughter

There is a rumbling flatbed truck
waiting in front of my house
whose driver is a small man
in an orange vest
holding a phone
and a breech loading rifle
filled with one great slug of lead

like a war horse and a buffalo guy
stopping before they plow down the road
trampling and shooting.

They want us with our troubles intact
and have cordoned off a corner
with stout rope and fixed stanchions
to keep us from bouncing off
when they hit the inevitable bumps.

I'm in my house, packing.
I have nothing in case of rain,
and since it is a truck
not a horse,
and a gun
not a dream,
there will be no hide.

The House Comes Down

You are accumulating
when the decline begins.

Gradually you can't hold any of it.
The beauty around you disappears.
There was a woman, there is no woman.

The dump truck you bought new
sinks into the ground beside another wreck.
Kids smash the headlights.

Bottles pile up. Bathroom fills with shit.
Roof gives way on the addition.
Snow gets in.
You haven't got the money.

Neighbors build and build.
You haven't got the energy.
Another leak, the rain finds you.
Because it's you, you don't care.

Your body is toxic.
Just one more drop, you say,
we're all going anyway,
you're not waiting.

Your only visitors are official.
You haven't got the will
to do it with a gun
or a bridge.

One day they take you away
because your lungs won't inhale

and you can't speak.
You think this is the end.

There's no one to tell the medics
to let you go
and you are revived.

When they leave,
you write on your forehead,
"Do not resuscitate."

Help Wanted

Lunatic:

A person, preferably fifty or older, to live in a small conservative town, where very little happens and everyone knows the others' business.

You will appear unannounced in places where you are not invited. You will mumble regularly and occasionally rave wise, often pithy, but mostly long rambling diatribes against the status quo. Drunkenness is allowed, but not required. Addiction is strictly prohibited.

We will provide an apartment behind the old stable that will be poorly heated in winter and overheated in summer. You will not mention its location to anyone, though it will be well known because you will not hide your comings or goings.

You will wear ill fitting designer clothing exclusively, until threadbare and ragged, though layering is permitted.

We prefer that you wash rarely and if male, that you grow a long beard, hopefully in a variety of graying colors, but we will definitely be unhappy if it is snowy white. Women should have long stringy hair. We don't want children to mistake you for Santa or Mrs. Claus, and if any misconception develops along those lines you will be dismissed.

We would prefer you to be childless, however, if you have children and are on good terms with them and must entertain them in your home, we'd like their visits to be brief and mysterious, so as to compound your legend.

We will pay all your essential living expenses, and a daily stipend, but that must be kept a complete secret or we will end it and deny having ever given you a cent. All payments will be in cash at unannounced places by unknown means and unnamed others. We encourage you to supplement your income panhandling money for wine, etc.

You must never tell a lie or shy away from controversial topics. You will go by a heartwarming name, like Old Man or Old Lady Johnson if you are white, or Brother or Sister Jackson if you are black. We'd rather you were not Latino, but if you meet all other criteria, we will hire you and would appreciate you going by the name Dr. Gus, which will eventually become known is the diminutive for your given name: Augusto or Augusta, as the case may be. Additionally, regardless of your race, we expect you to create confusion about your origin, European, African, South American, Central American, Asian. You could be any. You should be all, variously.

Asians are encouraged to apply, though we recognize the difficulty men may have growing a substantially imposing beard. Asian names should be a single letter, like Mr. G or Mrs. O and you should make references to the deep meaning of life. Facility in some martial art would be a plus.

Regardless of your race, we expect you to promote racial tension by raving about cultural inequity and supporting the cause of minorities, whether or not there are any in town. Even the miseries of middle class white men should be grist for your mill.

We expect you will also point up the ridiculous nature of people so as not to become a bore. Lunatics say the darnedest things. You are forbidden from taking a position in local politics and must never back a candidate for office. We encourage you to rail at religion, but be silent on the existence of God(s).

You will very occasionally be seen *apparently* defecating in public, though not often or verifiably enough to provoke a reaction by the authorities.

If a child or group of children attempts to befriend you, you will dissuade them using any means at your disposal up to and including humiliation. The children of this town lack humility. If a child or group of children attempts to hurt you, don't be surprised. Run away.

You will kowtow to no one, but defer to everyone and should you ever be drawn unwillingly into a fight, you will defend yourself with information that you gather in the course of your normal work day, which will consist of visiting all the public buildings and public spaces of the town. By public we also mean private places open to the public. You will appear at every place often, but never predictably and occasionally will not visit a place for weeks so that some people will become concerned for your whereabouts, if not your welfare or your life.

You may develop friendships in town, but we expect that those relationships will be kept sufficiently clouded to result in any personal information being obscure or at least vague.

We expect your tenure to be for life, though if you decide to quit, we expect you to disappear as secretly as you arrive and show yourself in several nearby towns as you exit.

Applicants must have a graduate degree, preferably a science related doctorate, be fluent in at least two languages, as well as Microsoft Office and any one of the leading email programs. All contact between the parties, except as provided above, will cease as soon as an applicant is chosen. Please send resumes to:

TheCommittee@SmallTownNews.ma.us.gov

The position will remain open until filled.

Extreme Unction (or My Captor's Hands)

After he starved me to the point of death,
I couldn't lift my body from the bed.

He came into the room and talked to me
in a warm water voice.

I was silent past fright.
One muscle keeping me.

He used his fingers
like legs, his palms to raise me.

I was a heartbeat in his hands
imagining love one last time.

Gladiator

On my foot,
heel to be more precise,
a posterior calcaneus lat left,
in layman's language—bone spur,
grows where my Achilles tendon is attached.
It burns like a spear.
Its fire pulls me up lame.

Almost always associated with Haglund's deformity,
it isn't rare; we limp around in legions.

I'm happy
because for most of human history
I would have already been eaten by lions.

Insomnia

When I was a boy
my father's factory burned to the ground
and a man died slowly, in agony.

Both men to blame,
it should have happened to neither.

That summer I dreamt that rain
had been falling for days,
covering thick grass with clear water,
creeping toward the foundation,
green mirror for the full moon
that rocked in the sky
and grew as it fell toward earth.

Restaurant Owner

A morose chef
has settled in my kitchen.
He sees no humor in my limp,
or the way I slosh his soup.
His wife has perpetual cancer.
His children are too many,
requiring the long form and specialists.
He's in the cellar
complaining about the windows
in all weather.
His pants are baggy where it doesn't matter.
He cooks what's left of my joy
in a giant pot filled with bitterness.
His bread is moldy.
His time is short.
His god is angry.
At night,
I cannot shake him.

Catching Up

She took the doctor to me,
and told him, "This is all he does now."

He took out his stethoscope,
which I enjoy against my chest,
the thump of his heavy thumb behind his hand,
the little taps below my kneecaps.

I said no, that I did many things
and would only write about all this later,
then left the room to write, things to catch up on.

Sinking

The tack from no to yes,
when you slip off guilt like another berth,
is a thought so slender it is the color of sky on water,
its weight, smoke on a tonnage scale,
its sails trimmed,

but you knew it was yes all along,
the struggle not with turning
but with saying,
as if every time the choice you make before
the bottle is as big as a ship
when in fact, no,
was smashed against your prow
and shattered a lifetime ago
when you set the course
for the unknown sea
and drank.

It's Simple

I like the quiet of gloves,
the humility of socks,
the cockiness of hats.

I like your hands,
your feet,
your head.

I like the way your eyes
empty out for me
and everything else disappears.

I Make Her Morning Coffee

When a long and happily married woman
talks about her husband,
what he'll do in any given situation,
there is no hope in it.
Not that he's hopeless,
only that she's given up thoughts of change,
of getting an unexpected effect,
a new line of thought,
a surprising consequence,
a different man.

It's possible,
of course,
but that is not her expectation.
Hope doesn't figure.

A long and happily married man
considers every woman
and every moment
a possibility.
He is full of hope
and chooses his wife
again and again and again.

Anticipation

When I was into my morning reading
she said something
that I left alone until afternoon
when I saw her plate,
yellow orange yolk,
crumb on the smears,
cup standing squat and empty,
pot of water on the stove.

I remembered the simmering,
saw her crack the shell,
pull the toast and slice strips,
dunking one after another,
sips of coffee between,
a simple eating rhythm,
tip of her tongue to the corner of her lips,
pushing her plate across the table,
crossing our rooms with a little hip tilt,
whispering close into my ear,
"There was nothing else to eat
so I soft boiled an egg."

Ferment

When I first walked among these vines
grapes hung everywhere,
ripe and embarrassed with yeast.

My voracious greed to harvest
ran to puddles of excess,
leaving fruit to turn to wine,
filling the empty cistern.

We Embers, We Cool Kisses

In our bed,
windows overhead,
there is news,
the night is rain;
old, silent, slouching,
or moonlight;
lost and found for t-shirts and panties,
her side, or mine.

We put our novels down
to non-fiction seminars in technique,
yes, yes, that's right...

or nights with no hints,
no clues,
only tinder,
easy kindling,
no test,
we burn,
we embers.

Come morning,
I leave
always my warm kisses
on her cool neck
between chin and clavicle
the place that fits my face.

What Isn't Said in the Ceremony

She'll become like the inside of the mask,
the place where your skin pushes against plastic,
high cheekbones of hate, which you can't hide,
flat forehead of sweat, which you must bear,
a parade of your own grotesques
floating under your eyelids
where you thought you were alone
or at least hoped that you were dreaming.

The vows exact a promise
that you'll attend in her duress,
but she's on a pair of mismatched stilts and prefers
the high one;
you no longer want to hike up her legs
and down,
you'll tire of laughing,
crying is out of the question,
the hill is still ahead.

She'll have been where you have been,
you'll trace your route in her wrinkles.

The transformation is the sacrament.
She wears the clothes you wear when you're naked
and she becomes you.
You become her.
She becomes you.

After the Hurricane

Years ago
from our porch
we hung a steel wind chime
whose keys barely touched,
each ping a surprise.

Two weeks after the storm,
the lengthening quiet reminds me
it needs re-stringing.

I've also been mute, listening
to the deep silence
waiting in the metal,
our unspoken words,
dangling.

I'd be tempted
to leave them unsaid
if the price wasn't music,
but I can't wait any longer
for her to sing
over the ringing in my ears.

Now, for making half this silence,
owning all these days of deafness
I'm penitent
because for all this time
I could have also been the breeze.

Palms

I want to feel your warm hands
patting my back,
gripping my arm,
rubbing my head,
all parts of the boy
fallen as far as a coconut
just as hard.

Supplicants

We play Yahtzee,
a game of chance,
none with the upper hand,
cupped black dots on spare white backs
sprinkled across a granite table.

Strategy a small role.
Choices matter,
periodically tricking us into believing
we will numbers and combinations.

We grow silent as they
clack at us,
rat tat on the rock altar,
rat tat, rat tat.

Bad Wine Waiting

She died. I quit.

My blood pump useless.

Stopped meals making.

My cloth frayed, worn.

Her seep not linger out open doors.

Our dog incontinent, lying down.

All over everywhere,
each sad mission,
no one waiting,
and bad wine drinking.

Ever meeting a stranger.

My only person.

Beach House

Table grapes.

Babies in basins.

Light at dusk moments before rain
swept by black and thunder
into summer closets.

Incandescent bulb
shining through cracks
and around doors,
rhythmic shadows.

Steamed ears of corn.

Clams on bed of seaweed
over hot round stones.

Grapes again.

Sun warmed puddles of rain
rinsed clear through soft green grass
between toes.

Sand all the way to vineyards.

Beads of water funneled into fruit.

Grapes!

Drunk Month

Once again August is gaudy
confirming what we all know
in our flowering minds,
bloated stomachs
and balled out lungs;
excess is ripe to rot,
endings are bittersweet better-offs,
harvest is a race.

Another Fall

On a brilliant fall morning
a shadow rushes to catch its leaf.
The resting pair trembles
amid all the little sounds of decay,
slow curling in the burn of days
that have already consumed summer.

Promise

Thicken the clouds,
lower the temp,
push back the moon,
chill the wind.

Shorten the days,
angle the sun,
darken the sky,
delay the dawn.

Lengthen the shade,
brittle the ground,
promise me nothing,
winter is come.

Children Have No Fear of Winter

Winter is an attic where old dresses are stored,
the storehouse where the other seasons are kept.

Winter is the year's subconscious
where much hard work gets done.

Winter prepares.
Every death a seed.

Overwintering Honeybees

The living huddle
against the shoulders of the dead,
rubbed with lingering smells of past lives,
ash and incense,
old bodies on the stoop,
another spent season,
another winter of white,
flecked with corpses,
no flying in or out,
the sun so low all the gold is a generation old,
fuel for the farewell ball
careful stores burned at a desperate feast,
until angled rays peel back into the hole
and the yellow and the black and the dust
of useless wings blow clear for spring.

Farm Hands

I lived through the year
there were no apples.

That spring there were buds,
and flowers, tiny fruit that froze solid
in twelve degrees after a hard rain.
What didn't break, rotted.

The trees raced to catch up.
All their missing leaves regrew.
More than a month behind,
they were off like a shot from a new starting block,
sprinting into a northern summer,
aiming to right themselves before fall frost,
new buds, new flowers, small fruit,
big green fruit,
looking in every way like money in the bank.

We counted and exhorted them
when just before maturity, it happened again:
Hard rain, twelve degrees,
almost every apple broken from its branch.

My mother cried. My father sobered.
I thought the pain we felt was for the trees.

The following year all the trees
in the orchard were more gnarled,
grayer with blacker knobs, sinewy fibers
lovely and strong like muscles on long-lived hands.

Full Circle

When his plumage turned from drab to gold
and the finch considered
nest or seed, a sudden urge compelled him
to fling it all aside and dance in flight
precisely at an angle to catch the brilliant sun
a dive and glide
he never knew he fancied
until he donned his father's clothes.

Come With Me to New Salem

We'll sit on a wall
thrown tumbled and straight
where trees anticipate
another season's cidering.

We'll fly like yellow jackets
from tree to under tree
getting drunk on drops
of McIntosh and Gravenstein.

We'll float
between black rock clouds
counting jays
in steam and passing rain.

We'll sleep
in the field hand's room
at the top of the house
where summer's heat survives.

We'll dream
the end of autumn
white as paper in our arms
as another winter flies.

Come stay with me 'til spring
at old South Main and Lovers Lane.

Halfway Home

I'll be your dead father
who you think about at times like now,
gone ahead where the road
takes a dip before the hill.

I'll walk faster than you,
call down from the top
lying about the effort,
knowing that once you've begun
you'll not want to turn back.

I'll tell you what's over the crest,
if it's as high as it looks,
or an illusion.

I'll tell you
from here I can see
miles in each direction,
all the hills we've passed,
a winding ribbon of road,
green forests and leafy overhangs,
But ahead!

You should see what's ahead!
Come up and take my hand
and if you're too tired
I'll throw you on my shoulders
because it all looks easy now,
all downhill as far as I can see.

This collection was set in Brioso Pro, designed by Robert Slimbach to evoke the immediacy and fluency of calligraphy.

33862051R00063

Made in the USA
Middletown, DE
31 July 2016